A
Woman
of
Genius

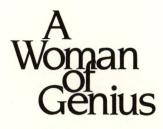

A Woman of Genius

The Intellectual Autobiography of
Sor Juana Inés de la Cruz

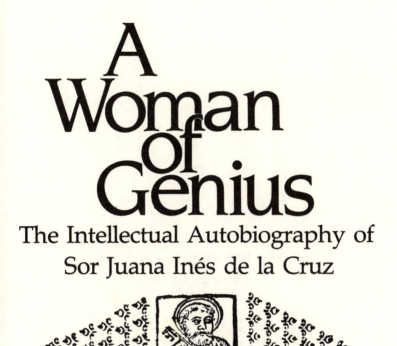

Translation and Introduction by
MARGARET SAYERS PEDEN

This edition contains some refinements in the translation of *La Respuesta* by Professor Peden, together with a
new appendix describing a recently discovered Sor
Juana letter written in 1681, ten years before *La Respuesta,* which adds new insights into her character and
personality.

Conceived and published by

Lime Rock Press, Inc.
an independent small press
Mount Riga Road,
Salisbury, Conn. 06068

INTRODUCTION
by
Margaret Sayers Peden

Sor Juana Inés de la Cruz was a Mexican nun of the Order of Saint Jerome, and a prolific writer of courtly and religious poetry, sacred and profane plays, personal essays, scholarly research, and religious treatises. In 1690, she had the audacity to set down in writing a critical attack on a sermon delivered forty years earlier by Antonio de Vieyra, a famed Portuguese Jesuit priest, "Sermon on the Mandate" [The washing of feet on Maunday Thursday].

Father de Vieyra's sermon (one of some six he had written on the subject) had addressed itself to the question of what Christ's greatest *fineza* — His greatest kindness, His greatest gift to mankind — may have been. In his argument de Vieyra negated the opinions of Saints Augustine, Thomas Aquinas, and Chrysostom. The Jesuit's contradicting "three Holy Fathers of the Church," as well as his arrogant claim that he would offer as example a "greater" kindness for each *fineza* posited by the saints, greatly offended Sor Juana. She discussed the sermon with friends among the religious community of Mexico City, later writing that her critique had its origin in the "prattle of a conversation." During one of these "conversations," some unidentified religious personage of authority expressed the wish to see her opinions on the sermon refined in writing. Sor Juana, responding to the person "whose authority could not be denied," complied, entitling the work *Critique of a Sermon*.

This *Critique* circulated from hand to hand and eventually came to the notice of Don Manuel Fernández de Santa Cruz y Sahagún, the Bishop of Puebla. The Bishop responded with two apparently contradictory, but ultimately interrelated, acts. Recognizing the importance of the document, he retitled it, calling it the *Carta Atenagórica,* or "Letter Worthy of Athena," and had it printed at his own expense. He sent a copy to Sor Juana with his personal dedication. At the same time, in a letter of November 2 , 1690, signed with the pseudonym Sor Filotea ("Lover of God"),he criticized Sor Juana for her actions and suggested that she dedicate herself to more suitable pursuits.

Though the general tone of his letter is amiable — "I, at least, have admired the liveliness of the concepts, the sagacity of the evidence, and the energetic clarity with which the matter is argued" — the Bishop also took advantage of the occasion to repeat comments circulating among Sor Juana's detractors, those jealous courtiers and clerics to whom Sor Juana would refer so bitterly in her subsequent *Response* ("La Respuesta"). "What a pity," the Bishop wrote, "that so great an intellect should lower itself in such a way by unworthy notice of the Earth that it have not desire to penetrate what transpires in Heaven; and, since it be already lowered to the ground, that it not descend further, to consider what transpires in Hell."

"Human letters," he added, "are slaves, and are wont to take advantage of the divine; and they must be censured when they steal from Divine Wisdom to give to human reason, making ladies of those intended to be servants. . ."

The Bishop of Puebla tempered his remonstrance by writing that while he did not concur with the "vulgarity" of those who would criticize "the employment of letters among women," he nevertheless agreed that, following the teachings of Saint Paul, *women should be content to study for the love of learning,* and not in order to teach. He reminded Sor Juana that she had "spent a great deal of time in the study of philosophers and poets," and counselled her to renounce these vain pursuits to turn her attention to perfecting her studies in the realm of the divine: "I do not intend, by this advice, that you alter your natural inclinations by renouncing books, but, rather, that you better them by reading occasionally in the book of Jesus Christ."

In part, the Bishop's counsel was contradictory, and some of his accusations unjust. The *Atenagórica* letter was in fact a theological treatise. The number of Sor Juana's poems written on religious themes far exceeds that of her profane love poems. She wrote various sacred *loas* [introductions to plays], and three *auto sacramentales* [religious plays], one of which, *The Divine Narcissus,* is particularly interesting for its unique combination of Greek and native Indian mythology. She had written religious "exercises" for the nuns' devotions. And her *villancicos* [religious carols]   had for several years been sung in the Bishop's own church in Puebla. The fact that the suggestion that she renounce human letters in favor of the divine came from her Bishop, and not from the lesser sources of attack to which she was accustomed, caused Sor Juana to acknowledge in *La Respuesta* that "though it comes in the guise of counsel, [it] will have for me the authority of a precept."

There can be no doubt that the Bishop's letter was a turning point in Sor Juana's life, as it was to become in the literary heritage of the Americas. Stung by the Bishop's admonitions, she mulled over the letter for several months, considering its implications, organizing her defenses. The obsession of her life, her quest for knowledge, was in jeopardy. Her very right to study had been questioned. Her reply to the Bishop, the *Response to the Most Illustrious Poetess Sor Filotea de la Cruz*, dated March 1, 1691, became the unburdening of years of repressed frustration.

La Respuesta, in its protest against the Bishop's injunctions, in its rebuttal of criticism occasioned by jealousy and envy, in its portrayal of a lifetime dedicated to learning and enlightenment, in its orderly defense of the rights of women to study and to teach, and in the glimpses of thinly-veiled anger and exquisitely-controlled irony which probably were not perceived in its time, is a unique document, what one critic has called a defense of the rights of women to education and culture that was to find no equal — in America or in Europe — for at least a century and a half.

Sor Juana's contemporaries were less tolerant of *La Respuesta*. Though the document was not published until after her death, it reached the hands, certainly, of those immediately surrounding Sor Juana. Her personal confessor, Father Antonio Núñez de Miranda, "withdrew his assistance." Her relationship with her Archbishop, Don Francisco de Aguiar y Seijas, whose aversion to women could only be described as pathological, further deteriorated.

La Respuesta, meanwhile, found its way to Spain and was included in the third volume of Sor Juana's works, *Fame and Posthumous Works of the Phoenix of Mexico, the Tenth Muse, Poetess of America*, published in Madrid in 1700. It has been included, in excerpt, or in its entirety, in every major Spanish-language anthology of Sor Juana's works since that time.

Almost three centuries have passed since Sor Juana's death in 1695. In spite of exhaustive research there are great lacunae in regard to her biography, the precise chronology of her works, the contents of her fabled personal library, and the intricacies of her personal relationships, that probably will never be filled in. The two principal sources for biographical information remain, after centuries, *La Respuesta* itself, and a brief biographical essay which borrows heavily from *La Respuesta* published in 1700 by Father Diego Calleja . These documents tell us that Juana was born on November 12, 1651, at eleven o'clock in the morning (although recently many scholars have accepted an earlier date, 1648). Her mother was Isabel Ramirez, who in her last will and testament confessed to having remained unwed, though the mother of six "natural" children. Her father was Pedro Manuel de Asbaje y Vargas Machuca, a Basque from the Province of Guipuzcoa. Juana was born in the shadow of the famous volcanos Popocateptl and Ixtacihuatl in the village of San Miguel de Nepantla (Nepantla is a native Nahuatl name meaning "land in the middle"), some sixty kilometers southeast of the City of Mexico. Father Calleja reports that Sor Juana was born in a rural home in a room called "The

Cell," an occurrence, he believes, that insured that "with her first breath she was enamored of monastic life and instructed that this was what life was about: to breathe the air of the cloister."

In 1669, at the age of 18, Sor Juana signed her profession of faith in the Convent of Saint Jerome in Mexico City as the "legitimate daughter" of Don Pedro de Asbaje y Vargas Machuca. Father Calleja , for obvious reasons, speaks of the "marriage" of her father and mother. But the evidence leaves little question that Sor Juana was an illegitimate child, and her birth must often have been the subject of palace gossip and a matter of concern to Sor Juana throughout her life.

Though Isabel Ramírez de Santillana had three daughters by Pedro de Asbaje, Sor Juana knew very little of her father. For a time, the father's role was filled by her maternal grandfather, Don Pedro Ramírez de Santillana. This was undoubtedly a most fortunate relationship, and provided one of the few visible and rational sources for the amazing intellect of this greatly talented woman, for Juana's grandfather is reported to have been an indefatigable reader, a man whose house held tables spilling over with books. There the young Juana could satisfy her natural inclinations. She refers in *La Respuesta* to her grandfather's library, telling how when her mother refused to allow her to dress as a boy and go to Mexico City to study, "I assuaged my disappointment by reading the many and varied books belonging to my grandfather."

In *La Respuesta*, Sor Juana recounts her early love of learning: how at three, without her mother's knowledge,

she learned to read; how she tormented her mother to allow her to go to Mexico City; how, in fact, at the age of eight, she did go to the city to live with her mother's sister María, and María's well-established husband Juan de Mata; how once in Mexico City she undertook her studies in earnest, learning Latin in some twenty sessions; how she continued to pursue her interests in every field of knowledge. From Father Calleja we learn how the court and the intellectual community of that city were astounded by Juana's learning, and enchanted by her beauty.

Father Calleja adds substantially to our store of knowledge, though he is occasionally prone to error (he writes, for instance, that Juana went to live with her grandfather in Mexico City.) Calleja tells us that Juana Inés won her first prize — not surprisingly, a book — at the age of eight, when she composed a *loa* for the Festival of the most Holy Sacrament being celebrated in the church of nearby Amecameca. Her impact on the royal court in Mexico City is attested to by the former Viceroy of Mexico, His Excellency the Marqués de Mancera, who in his later years personally reported to Calleja that "the Señora Vicereine could live scarcely a moment without her Juana Inés." The Marquéz also told Calleja how he convoked (possibly at the instigation of those who held less than affection for the admiration lavished on a young girl from the provinces) a body of some forty learned men — theologians, philosophers, mathematicians, historians, poets, and humanists, among others — to examine the child who had so astounded the court with her erudition and her poetry. Juana was sixteen. Calleja quotes Mancera

as saying that "in the manner that a royal galleon might fend off the attacks of small canoes, so did Juana extricate herself from the questions, arguments, and objections these many men, each in his speciality, directed to her."

Fame and adulation, along with their concommitant envy and jealousy, were to follow Sor Juana through the remainder of her life. Gifted with intelligence, grace, and great beauty, she continued to be a favorite of a succession of Viceroys and their ladies, even after taking her vows as a nun. Her convent cell served for many years as a center of court activity. It is probable that most of her love poems were composed at the request of the members of court society. We know, for example, that the Laura, and the Lysi or Filis, poems are addressed to the Vicereines, the Marquesa de Mancera, and the Condesa de Paredes.

In the light of her warm reception at court, many critics have speculated as to the reasons that led Sor Juana to enter the convent. Why did she not marry? Was a fitting marriage denied her because of her illegitimacy? Did she have a true calling for the religious life? Did she suffer a disastrous love affair — some see evidence for this in a series of poems addressed to Fabio — which drove her to take the vows? The answer will surely never be determined with certainty. The most convincing argument is given by Sor Juana herself in *La Respuesta*. Given the "total antipathy she felt for marriage," she writes — though she does not clarify the reasons for that repugnance — she deemed convent life "the least unsuitable and the most honorable" she could elect.

Sor Juana was truly a *sorpresa*, one student of her work has said. First, there is the eternal "surprise" of her genius. But she was also a *sor presa*, a captive nun, because in her time only the convent offered a woman an opportunity to pursue an intellectual life. This is the simplest and most direct answer to the question: her desire to study led her to the cloister. She continued to study until the spiritual crisis provoked by the publication of the *Atenagórica* letter and "Sor Filotea's" remonstrances.

In the history of Spanish American literature, Sor Juana stands alone, the prodigy of the colonial period, her genius uncontested today. She is the Mexican muse, the inspiration of contemporary writers. She has not always been held in such esteem.

The seventeenth and twentieth centuries form a kind of parenthesis around a long period of silence in Sor Juana criticism and appreciation, for neo-classical tastes relegated the baroque in general, and Sor Juana — the epitome of the colonial baroque — in particular, to an age of oblivion. It was the reemergence of interest in the baroque on the part of German scholars in the second half of the nineteenth century that opened the way to a revival of interest in Sor Juana. But it is only in the twentieth century, beginning in the 'twenties, intensifying in the 'thirties and 'forties, proliferating in the 'fifties, and continuing unabated today, that this literary interest became significant.

Sor Juana, like every great writer, has been subjected to a succession of critical modes. One area of criticism, largely justified, is related to the excesses of the baroque in

her work. She is often accused of having surpassed her peninsular model, the Spanish poet Luis de Góngora y Argote, in inaccessibility. Julio Jimenez Rueda probably best expresses this view when he says, "The versification in Sor Juana's works is natural and clear when it is sincere. When she imitates Góngora her poetry is motley and in bad taste. . . ." But when Sor Juana's own voice is raised, — a voice which Mexico's dean of letters, Don Alfonso Reyes, has called "that impetuous, dionysiac lyricism à la divine," — it transcends time and place to become universal.

Sor Juana's critics have attempted to penetrate the complexities of her person in a flood of psychological and psychoanalytical studies that range from the dubious to the ludicrous. She is variously portrayed as a true mystic, and as a cunning, hypocritical heretic who managed to dupe both the Jesuits and the Inquisition. One critic writes that her tragedy was to have been born a woman, never having been meant to be one, while another refers to the gentleness of her feminine heart, always the beloved, the mother.

Pages of speculation have been printed about her love poems: did she experience carnal love? Who was Fabio, who did not return her love? Who was Silvio, whose love for her was unrequited? Such speculation seems little likely to be resolved. Many of the poems addressed to Paula and Lysi (the Marquesa de Mancera and the Condesa de Paredes) can be read as love poems, and yet no one has suggested a relationship beyond friendship between these women and Sor Juana. The most sensible interpretation, in the absence of any conclusive

evidence as to whether hers were real or imagined love affairs, would be to accept Fabio and Silvio, along with the Alcinos, Celios, and Cloris of her poems, as conventions of the time.

Between 19 1 and 1957, Alfonso Méndez Plancarte published the basic source book for Sor Juana scholars, a four volume edition of her complete works. Here, in a modern edition, we witness the scope and variety of Sor Juana's writing. Plays, poems, prose. The lyric, the panegyric, the satire. A series of *villancicos* written in praise of Saint Catherine of Alexandria, a woman for whom Sor Juana seems to have felt a particular affinity. A series of verses for the Feast of the Assumption written in Negro dialect. A *tocotín,* or country dance, written entirely in native Nahuatl. Poems containing a mixture of Spanish, Latin, and Nahuatl, or Latin and Negro dialect. Some of the finest sonnets in the Spanish language. An almost impenetrably baroque description of a triumphal arch constructed in honor of the arrival of a new Viceroy. A fragment of a treatise on music. "First Dream," Sor Juana's master work, a long poem not truly appreciated until this century, a beautiful lyric, but also an epistemological inquiry that anticipated the Enlightenment. The *Atenagórica* letter. *La Respuesta.*

North American readers may gain some perspective on this amazing talent if we consider that when Sor Juana was enjoying the adulation of an elegant court, the Plymouth Colony had been in existence for fewer than fifty years. Sor Juana had written plays, had had her plays performed, and had been urged by her confessor to cease

writing plays — all nearly a hundred years before the first play by a North American writer had been given a professional performance in the United States. The only woman who figured in North American colonial literature, Anne Bradstreet — actually English, not American by birth — cannot be compared to Sor Juana. Other than the novelty of *being* women, these writers share in common only a charming coincidence: the fact that both were called by contemporaries "the tenth Muse." (In Spanish, la *décima musa* has an additional resonance. The *décima* is a commonly-used verse form. Sor Juana was "the *décima* Muse," who also wrote *décimas*.)

In her *Respuesta* to "Sor Filotea," Sor Juana said that she would not again "take up my pen" in defense against her attackers. She did not. There were a few "scribblings." She responded, for example, to praise resulting from the publication of the first two volumes of her works. She composed a few lines to the Conde de Galve and his lady. But the outpouring of *La Respuesta* had drained Sor Juana. Her spirit was subdued. She turned more and more to her religious duties.

Sor Juana now composed three documents renewing her vows and reaffirming her faith in the Immaculate Conception of the Virgin Mary. One of these professions she signed in her own blood. Her late portraits show her wearing on her breast the ornament that was a traditional part of the habit of her order, a large oval representation of the Annunciation.

But the clearest evidence of her resignation is to be found in the dispersement of her library. Parting with her beloved books must have been the most painful act of Sor

Juana's life. Some have speculated that the number of volumes contained in her library may have been as high as four thousand. This seems unlikely, since this is almost the total number of books imported into New Spain during Sor Juana's lifetime. But it was a famous collection. We can see some of the titles in one of the best-known of her portraits, but no catalogue has survived — one of the true losses of literary history. Father Calleja saw the process of separation from her books as movement toward a more spiritual phase of her life. As the "true dawn" was approaching, he writes, "she considered artificial illumination unnecessary." A few of the books were retained in the convent for the use of her sisters, but most were sold, along with her collection of musical and mathematical instruments. The proceeds were distributed among the poor.

On April 17, 1695, at 4:00 o'clock in the morning, four years after writing *La Respuesta* and forty-four years, five months, five days, and five hours after her birth, Sor Juana Inés de la Cruz — Juana Ramírez de Asbaje, as she referred to herself — died while nursing her sister nuns during a virulent, but unidentified, plague.

Although almost three hundred years have passed since her death, only a few of the hundreds of Sor Juana's poems, prose pieces, and plays are available outside Spanish-language literature.

This volume is believed to be the first complete English translation of Sor Juana's prose masterpiece. It is hoped that with its publication a window will be opened onto the work of this remarkably gifted woman of genius.

$\mathcal{M}$y most illustrious *señora*, dear lady. It has not been my will, my poor health, or my justifiable apprehension that for so many days delayed my response. How could I write, considering that at my very first step my clumsy pen encountered two obstructions in its path? The first (and, for me, the most uncompromising) is to know how to reply to your most learned, most prudent, most holy, and most loving letter. For I recall that when Saint Thomas, the Angelic Doctor of Scholasticism, was asked about his silence regarding his teacher Al-

Muy ilustre Señora, mi Señora: No mi voluntad, mi poca salud y mi justo temor han suspendido tantos días mi respuesta. ¿Qué mucho si, al primer paso, encontraba para tropezar mi torpe pluma dos imposibles? El primero (y para mí el más riguroso) es saber responder a vuestra doctísima, discretísima, santísima y amorosísima carta. Y si veo que preguntado el Ángel de las Escuelas, Santo Tomás, de su silencio con Alberto Magno, su maestro, respondió que callaba porque nada sabía decir digno de Alberto, con cuánta mayor razón no

bertus Magnus, he replied that he had not spoken because he knew no words worthy of Albertus. With so much greater reason, must not I too be silent? Not, like the Saint, out of humility, but because in reality I know nothing I can say that is worthy of you. The second obstruction is to know how to express my appreciation for a favor as unexpected as extreme, for having my scribblings printed, a gift so immeasurable as to surpass my most ambitious aspiration, my most fervent desire, which even as an entity of reason never entered my thoughts. Yours was a kindness, finally, of such magnitude that words cannot express my gratitude, a kindness exceeding the bounds of appreciation, as great as it was unexpected — which is as Quintilian said: *aspirations engender minor glory; benefices, major.*[1] To such a degree as to impose silence on the receiver.

When the blessedly sterile — that she might miraculously become fecund — Mother of John the Baptist saw in her house such an extraordinary visitor as the Mother of the Word, her reason became clouded and her speech deserted her; and thus, in the place of thanks, she burst out with doubts and questions: *And whence is to me [that the mother of my Lord should come to me?]*[2] And whence cometh such a thing to *me*? And so also it fell to Saul when he found himself the chosen, the annointed, King of Israel: *Am I not a son of Jemini, of the least tribe of Israel, and my kindred the last among all the families of the tribe of Benjamin? Why then hast thou spoken this word to me?*[3] And thus say I, most honorable lady. Why do I receive such favor? By chance, am I other than an humble nun, the lowliest creature of the world, the most unworthy to occupy your attention? "Wherefore then speakest thou so to me?" "And whence is this to me?" Nor to the first obstruction do I have any response other than I am little worthy of your eyes; nor to the second, other than wonder, in the stead of thanks, saying that I am not capable of thanking you for the smallest part of that which I owe you. This is not pretended

callaría, no como el Santo de humildad, sino que la realidad es no saber algo digno de vos. El segundo imposible es saber agradeceros tan excesivo como no esperado favor de dar a las prensas mis borrones; merced tan sin medida que aun se le pasara por alto a la esperanza más ambiciosa y al deseo más fantástico, y que ni aun como ente de razón pudiera caber en mis pensamientos; y, en fin, de tal magnitud que no sólo no se puede estrechar a lo limitado de las voces, pero excede a la capacidad del agradecimiento, tanto por grande como por no esperado, que es lo que dijo Quintiliano: *Minorem spei, maiorem benefacti gloriam pereunt* . Y tal, que enmudecen al beneficiado.

Cuando la felizmente estéril, para ser milagrosamente fecundada, madre del Bautista vio en su casa tan desproporcionada visita como la Madre del Verbo, se le entorpeció el entendimiento y se le suspendió el discurso; y así, en vez de agradecimientos, prorrumpió en dudas y preguntas: *Et unde hoc mihi?* ¿De dónde a mí viene tal cosa? Lo mismo sucedió a Saúl cuando se vio electo y ungido rey de Israel: *Numquid non filius Iemini ego sum de minima tribu Israel, et cognatio mea novissima inter omnes de tribu Beniamin? Quare igitur locutus es mihi sermonem istum?* . Así yo diré: ¿de dónde, venerable Señora, de dónde a mí tanto favor? ¿Por ventura soy más que una pobre monja, la más mínima criatura del mundo y la más indigna de ocupar vuestra atención? Pues *quare locutus es mihi sermonem istum? Et unde hoc mihi?*

Ni al primer imposible tengo más que responder que no ser nada digno de vuestros ojos; ni al segundo más que admiraciones, en vez de gracias, diciendo que no soy capaz de agradeceros la más mínima parte de lo que os debo. No es afectada modestia, Señora, sino ingenua verdad de toda mi alma, que al llegar a mis manos, impresa, la carta que vuestra propiedad llamó

17

modesty, lady, but the simplest truth issuing from the depths of my heart, that when the letter which with propriety you called *Atenagórica* reached my hands, in print, I burst into tears of confusion (withal, that tears do not come easily to me) because it seemed to me that your favor was but a remonstrance God made against the wrong I have committed, and that in the same way He corrects others with punishment He wishes to subject me with benefices, with this special favor for which I know myself to be His debtor, as for an infinitude of others from His boundless kindness. I looked upon this favor as a particular way to shame and confound me, it being the most exquisite means of castigation, that of causing me, by my own intellect, to be the judge who pronounces sentence and who denounces my ingratitude. And thus, when here in my solitude I think on these things, I am wont to say: Blessed art Thou, oh Lord, for Thou hast not chosen to place in the hands of others my judgment, nor yet in mine, but hast reserved that to Thy own, and freed me from myself, and from the necessity to sit in judgment on myself, which judgment, forced from my own intellect, could be no less than condemnation, but Thou hast reserved me to Thy mercy, because Thou lovest me more than I can love myself.

I beg you, lady, to forgive this digression to which I was drawn by the power of truth, and, if I am to confess all the truth, I shall confess that I cast about for some manner by which I might flee the difficulty of a reply, and was sorely tempted to take refuge in silence. But as silence is a negative thing, though it explains a great deal through the very stress of not explaining, we must assign some meaning to it that we may understand what the silence is intended to say, for if not, silence will say nothing, as that is its very office: *to say nothing*. The holy Chosen Vessel, Saint Paul, having been caught up into paradise, and having heard the arcane secrets of God, *heard secret words, which it is not granted to man to utter.*[4] He does not say what he

Atenagórica, prorrumpí (con no ser esto en mí muy fácil) en lágrimas de confusión, porque me pareció que vuestro favor no era más que una reconvención que Dios hace a lo mal que le correspondo; y que como a otros corrige con castigos, a mí me quiere reducir a fuerza de beneficios. Especial favor de que conozco ser su deudora, como de otros infinitos de su inmensa bondad; pero también especial modo de avergonzarme y confundirme: que es más primoroso medio de castigar hacer que yo misma, con mi conocimiento, sea el juez que me sentencie y condene mi ingratitud. Y así, cuando esto considero acá a mis solas, suelo decir: Bendito seáis vos, Señor, que no sólo no quisisteis en manos de otra criatura el juzgarme, y que ni aun en la mía lo pusisteis, sino que lo reservasteis a la vuestra, y me librasteis a mí de mí y de la sentencia que yo mismo me daría—que, forzada de mi propio conocimiento, no pudiera ser menos que de condenación—, y vos la reservasteis a vuestra misericordia, porque me amáis más de lo que yo me puedo amar.

Perdonad, Señora mía, la digresión que me arrebató la fuerza de la verdad; y si la he de confesar toda, también es buscar efugios para huir la dificultad de responder, y casi me he determinado a dejarlo al silencio; pero como éste es cosa negativa, aunque explica mucho con el énfasis de no explicar, es necesario ponerle algún breve rótulo para que se entienda lo que se pretende que el silencio diga; y si no, dirá nada el silencio, porque ése es su propio oficio: decir nada. Fue arrebatado el Sagrado Vaso de Elección al tercer Cielo, y habiendo visto los arcanos secretos de Dios, dice: *Audivit arcana Dei, quae non licet homini loqui* . No dice lo que vio, pero dice que no lo puede decir; de manera que aquellas cosas que no se pueden decir, es menester decir siquiera que no se pueden decir, para que se entienda que el callar no es no haber qué

heard; he says that he cannot say it. So that of things one cannot say, it is needful to say at least that they cannot be said, so that it may be understood that not speaking is not the same as having nothing to say, but rather being unable to express the many things there are to say. Saint John says that if all the marvels our Redeemer wrought "were written every one, the world itself, I think, would not be able to contain the books that should be written."[5] And Vieyra says on this point that in this single phrase the Evangelist said more than in all else he wrote; and this same Lusitanian Phoenix speaks well (but when does he not speak well, even when he does not speak well of others?) because in those words Saint John said everything left unsaid and expressed all that was left to be expressed. And thus I, lady, shall respond only that I do not know how to respond; I shall thank you in saying only that I am incapable of thanking you; and I shall say, through the indication of what I leave to silence, that it is only with the confidence of one who is favored and with the protection of one who is honorable that I presume to address your magnificence, and if this be folly, be forgiving of it, for folly may be good fortune, and in this manner I shall provide further occasion for your benignity and you will better shape my intellect.

Because he was halting of speech, Moses thought himself unworthy to speak with Pharoah, but after he found himself highly favored of God, and thus inspired, he not only spoke with God Almighty but dared ask the impossible: *shew me thy face.*[6] In this same manner, lady, and in view of how you favor me, I no longer see as impossible the obstructions I posed in the beginning: for who was it who had my letter printed unbeknownst to me? Who entitled it, who bore the cost, who honored it, it being so unworthy in itself, and in its author? What will such a person not do, not pardon? What would he fail to do, or fail to pardon? And thus, based on the supposition that I speak under the safe-conduct of your favor, and with the assurance of your

decir, sino no caber en las voces lo mucho que hay que decir. Dice San Juan que si hubiera de escribir todas las maravillas que obró nuestro Redentor, no cupieran en todo el mundo los libros; y dice Vieyra [6], sobre este lugar, que en sola esta cláusula dijo más el Evangelista que en todo cuanto escribió; y dice muy bien el Fénix Lusitano (pero ¿cuándo no dice bien, aun cuando no dice bien?), porque aquí dice San Juan todo lo que dejó de decir y expresó lo que dejó de expresar. Así yo, Señora mía, sólo responderé que no sé qué responder; sólo agradeceré diciendo que no soy capaz de agradeceros; y diré, por breve rótulo de lo que dejo al silencio, que sólo con la confianza de favorecida y con los valimientos de honrada me puedo atrever a hablar con vuestra grandeza. Si fuere necedad, perdonadla, pues es alhaja de la dicha, y en ella ministraré yo más materia a vuestra benignidad y vos daréis mayor forma a mi reconocimiento.

No se hallaba digno Moisés, por balbuciente, para hablar con Faraón, y después, el verse tan favorecido de Dios, le infunde tales alientos, que no sólo habla con el mismo Dios, sino que se atreve a pedirle imposibles: *Ostende mihi faciem tuam* [7]. Pues así yo, Señora mía, ya no me parecen imposibles los que puse al principio, a vista de lo que me favorecéis; porque quien hizo imprimir la Carta tan sin noticia mía, quien la intituló, quien la costeó, quien la honró tanto (siendo de todo indigna por sí y por su autora), ¿qué no hará?, ¿qué no perdonará?, ¿qué dejará de hacer y que dejará de perdonar? Y así, debajo del supuesto de que hablo con el salvoconducto de vuestros favores y debajo del seguro de vuestra benignidad, y de que me

benignity, and with the knowledge that like a second Aha-suerus you have offered to me to kiss the top of the golden scepter of your affection as a sign of conceding to me your benevolent license to speak and offer judgments in your exalted presence, I say to you that I have taken to heart your most holy admonition that I apply myself to the study of the Sacred Books, which, though it comes in the guise of counsel, will have for me the authority of a precept, but with the not insignificant consolation that even before your counsel I was disposed to obey your pastoral suggestion, as your direction, which may be inferred from the premise and arguments of my Letter. For I know well that your most sensible warning is not directed against it, but rather against those worldly matters of which I have written. And thus I had hoped with the Letter to make amends for any lack of application you may (with great reason) have inferred from others of my writings; and, speaking more particularly, I confess to you with all the candor of which you are deserving, and with the truth and clarity which are the natural custom in me, that my not having written often of sacred matters was not caused by disaffection or by want of application, but by the abundant fear and reverence due those Sacred Letters, knowing myself incapable of their comprehension and unworthy of their employment. Always resounding in my ears, with no little horror, I hear God's threat and prohibition to sinners like myself. *Why dost thou declare my justices, and take my covenant in thy mouth?*[7] This question, as well as the knowledge that even learned men are forbidden to read the Canticle of Canticles until they have passed thirty years of age, or even Genesis — the latter for its obscurity; the former in order that the sweetness of those epithalamia not serve as occasion for imprudent youth to transmute their meaning into carnal emotion, as borne out by my exalted Father Saint Jerome, who ordered that these be the last verses to be studied, and for the same reason: *And finally, one may read without peril*

habéis, como otro Asuero, dado a besar la punta del cetro de oro de vuestro cariño en señal de concederme benévola licencia para hablar y proponer en vuestra venerable presencia, digo que recibo en mi alma vuestra santísima amonestación de aplicar el estudio a Libros Sagrados, que aunque viene en traje de consejo, tendrá para mí sustancia de precepto; con no pequeño consuelo de que aun antes parece que prevenía mi obediencia vuestra pastoral insinuación, como a vuestra dirección, inferido del asunto y pruebas de la misma Carta. Bien conozco que no cae sobre ella vuestra cuerdísima advertencia, sino sobre lo mucho que habréis visto de asuntos humanos que he escrito; y así, lo que he dicho no es más que satisfaceros con ella a la falta de aplicación que habréis inferido (con mucha razón) de otros escritos míos. Y hablando con más especialidad os confieso, con la ingenuidad que ante vos es debida y con la verdad y claridad que en mí siempre es natural y costumbre, que el no haber escrito mucho de asuntos sagrados no ha sido desafición, ni de aplicación la falta, sino sobra de temor y reverencia debida a aquellas Sagradas Letras, para cuya inteligencia yo me conozco tan incapaz y para cuyo manejo soy tan indigna; resonándome siempre en los oídos, con no pequeño horror, aquella amenaza y prohibición del Señor a los pecadores como yo: *Quare tu enarras iustitias meas, et assumis testamentum meum per os tuum?* ; esta pregunta, y el ver que aun a los varones doctos se prohibía el leer los Cantares hasta que pasaban de treinta años, y aun el Génesis: éste por su oscuridad, y aquéllos porque de la dulzura de aquellos epitalamios no tomase ocasión la imprudente juventud de mudar el sentido en carnales afectos. Compruébalo mi gran Padre San Jerónimo, mandando que sea esto lo último que se estudie, por la misma razón: *Ad ultimum sine periculo discat Canti-*

the Song of Songs, for if it is read early one may suffer harm through not understanding those Epithalamia of the spiritual wedding which is expressed in carnal terms.[8] And Seneca says: *In the early years the faith is dim.*[9] For how then would I have dared take in my unworthy hands these verses, defying gender, age, and, above all, custom? And thus I confess that many times this fear has plucked my pen from my hand and has turned my thoughts back toward the very same reason from which they had wished to be born: which obstacle did not impinge upon profane matters, for a heresy against art is not punished by the Holy Office but by the judicious with derision, and by critics with censure, and censure, *just or unjust, is not to be feared,*[10] as it does not forbid the taking of communion or hearing of mass, and offers me little or no cause for anxiety, because in the opinion of those who defame my art, I have neither the obligation to know nor the aptitude to triumph. If, then, I err, I suffer neither blame nor discredit: I suffer no blame, as I have no obligation; no discredit, as I have no possibility of triumphing — *and no one is obliged to do the impossible.*[11] And, in truth, I have written nothing except when compelled and constrained, and then only to give pleasure to others; not alone without pleasure of my own, but with absolute repugnance, for I have never deemed myself one who has any worth in letters or the wit necessity demands of one who would write; and thus my customary response to those who press me, above all in sacred matters, is, what capacity of reason have I? what application? what resources? what rudimentary knowledge of such matters beyond that of the most superficial scholarly degrees? Leave these matters to those who understand them; I wish no quarrel with the Holy Office, for I am ignorant, and I tremble that I may express some proposition that will cause offense or twist the true meaning of some scripture. I do not study to write, even less to teach — which in one like myself were unseemly pride — but only to the end that if I

cum Canticorum, ne si in exordio legerit, sub carna-
libus verbis spiritualium nuptiarum Epithalamium non
intelligens, vulneretur ; y Séneca dice: *Teneris in*
annis haut clara est fides . Pues ¿cómo me atreviera
yo a tomarlo en mis indignas manos, repugnándolo el
sexo, la edad y, sobre todo, las costumbres? Y así confieso que muchas veces este temor me ha quitado la
pluma de la mano y ha hecho retroceder los asuntos
hacia el mismo entendimiento de quien querían bro-
tar; el cual inconveniente no topaba en los asuntos
profanos, pues una herejía contra el arte no la castiga
el Santo Oficio, sino los discretos con risa y los críti-
cos con censura; y ésta, *iusta vel iniusta, timenda non*
est , pues deja comulgar y oír misa, por lo cual me
da poco o ningún cuidado; porque, según la misma de-
cisión de los que lo calumnian, ni tengo obligación para
saber ni aptitud para acertar; luego si lo yerro, ni es
culpa ni es descrédito. No es culpa, porque no tengo
obligación; no es descrédito, pues no tengo posibi-
lidad de acertar, y *ad impossibilia nemo tenetur* .
Y, a la verdad, yo nunca he escrito sino violentada y forzada y sólo por dar gusto a otros; no sólo sin compla-
cencia, sino con positiva repugnancia, porque nunca
he juzgado de mí que tenga el caudal de letras e ingenio que pide la obligación de quien escribe; y así, es
la ordinaria respuesta a los que me instan, y más si
es asunto sagrado: «¿Qué entendimiento tengo yo, qué
estudio, qué materiales, ni qué noticias para eso, sino
cuatro bachillerías superficiales? Dejen eso para quien
lo entienda, que yo no quiero ruido con el Santo Oficio,
que soy ignorante y tiemblo de decir alguna proposi-
ción malsonante o torcer la genuina inteligencia de
algún lugar. Yo no estudio para escribir, ni menos
para enseñar (que fuera en mí desmedida soberbia),

study, I will be ignorant of less. This is my response, and these are my feelings.

I have never written of my own choice, but at the urging of others, to whom with reason I might say, *You have compelled me.*[12] But one truth I shall not deny (first, because it is well-known to all, and second, because although it has not worked in my favor, God has granted me the mercy of loving truth above all else), which is that from the moment I was first illuminated by the light of reason, my inclination toward letters has been so vehement, so overpowering, that not even the admonitions of others — and I have suffered many — nor my own meditations — and they have not been few — have been sufficient to cause me to forswear this natural impulse that God placed in me: the Lord God knows why, and for what purpose. And He knows that I have prayed that He dim the light of my reason, leaving only that which is needed to keep His Law, for there are those who would say that all else is unwanted in a woman, and there are even those who would hold that such knowledge does injury. And my Holy Father knows too that as I have been unable to achieve this (my prayer has not been answered), I have sought to veil the light of my reason — along with my name — and to offer it up only to Him who bestowed it upon me, and He knows that none other was the cause for my entering into Religion, notwithstanding that the spiritual exercises and company of a community were repugnant to the freedom and quiet I desired for my studious endeavors. And later, in that community, the Lord God knows — and, in the world, only the one who must know — how diligently I sought to obscure my name, and how this was not permitted, saying it was temptation: and so it would have been. If it were in my power, lady, to repay you in some part what I owe you, it might be done by telling you this thing which has never before passed my lips, except to be spoken to the one who should hear it. It is my hope that by having opened wide to you

sino sólo por ver si con estudiar ignoro menos.» Así lo respondo y así lo siento.

El escribir nunca ha sido dictamen propio, sino fuerza ajena; que les pudiera decir con verdad: *Vos me coegistis* . Lo que sí es verdad que no negaré (lo uno porque es notorio a todos, y lo otro porque, aunque sea contra mí, me ha hecho Dios la merced de darme grandísimo amor a la verdad) es que desde que me rayó la primera luz de la razón, fue tan vehemente y poderosa la inclinación a las letras, que ni ajenas reprensiones—que he tenido muchas—, ni propias reflejas —que he hecho no pocas—, han bastado a que deje de seguir este natural impulso que Dios puso en mí: Su Majestad sabe por qué y para qué; y sabe que le he pedido que apague la luz de mi entendimiento dejando sólo lo que baste para guardar su Ley, pues lo demás sobra, según algunos, en una mujer; y aun hay quien diga que daña. Sabe también Su Majestad que no consiguiendo esto, he intentado sepultar con mi nombre mi entendimiento, y sacrificárselo sólo a quien me lo dio; y que no otro motivo me entró en religión, no obstante que al desembarazo y quietud que pedía mi estudiosa intención eran repugnantes los ejercicios y compañía de una comunidad; y después, en ella, sabe el Señor, y lo sabe en el mundo quien sólo lo debió saber , lo que intenté en orden a esconder mi nombre, y que no me lo permitió, diciendo que era tentación; y sí sería. Si yo pudiera pagaros algo de lo que os debo, Señora mía, creo que sólo os pagara en contaros esto, pues no ha salido de mi boca jamás, excepto para quien debió salir . Pero quiero que con haberos franqueado de par en par las puertas de mi corazón, haciéndoos patentes sus más sellados secretos, conozcáis que no desdice de mi confianza lo

the doors of my heart, by having made patent to you its most deeply-hidden secrets, you will deem my confidence not unworthy of the debt I owe to your most august person and to your most uncommon favors.

Continuing the narration of my inclinations, of which I wish to give you a thorough account, I will tell you that I was not yet three years old when my mother determined to send one of my elder sisters to learn to read at a school for girls we call the *Amigas*. Affection, and mischief, caused me to follow her, and when I observed how she was being taught her lessons I was so inflamed with the desire to know how to read, that deceiving — for so I knew it to be — the mistress, I told her that my mother had meant for me to have lessons too. She did not believe it, as it was little to be believed, but, to humor me, she acceded. I continued to go there, and she continued to teach me, but now, as experience had disabused her, with all seriousness; and I learned so quickly that before my mother knew of it I could already read, for my teacher had kept it from her in order to reveal the surprise and reap the reward at one and the same time. And I, you may be sure, kept the secret, fearing that I would be whipped for having acted without permission. The woman who taught me, may God bless and keep her, is still alive and can bear witness to all I say. I also remember that in those days, my tastes being those common to that age, I abstained from eating cheese because I had heard that it made one slow of wits, for in me the desire for learning was stronger than the desire for eating — as powerful as that is in children. When later, being six or seven, and having learned how to read and write, along with all the other skills of needlework and household arts that girls learn, it came to my attention that in Mexico City there were Schools, and a University, in which one studied the sciences. The moment I heard this, I began to plague my mother with insistent and importunate pleas: she should dress me in boy's clothing and send me to Mexico City to

que debo a vuestra venerable persona y excesivos favores.

Prosiguiendo en la narración de mi inclinación, de que os quiero dar entera noticia, digo que no había cumplido los tres años de mi edad cuando enviando mi madre a una hermana mía, mayor que yo, a que se enseñase a leer en una de las que llaman Amigas , me llevó a mí tras ella el cariño y la travesura; y viendo que la daban lección, me encendí yo de manera en el deseo de saber leer, que engañando, a mi parecer, a la maestra, la dije que mi madre ordenaba me diese lección. Ella no lo creyó, porque no era creíble; pero, por complacer al donaire, me la dio. Proseguí yo en ir y ella prosiguió en enseñarme, ya no de burlas, porque la desengañó la experiencia; y supe leer en tan breve tiempo, que ya sabía cuando lo supo mi madre, a quien la maestra lo ocultó por darle el gusto por entero y recibir el galardón por junto; y yo lo callé, creyendo que me azotarían por haberlo hecho sin orden. Aún vive la que me enseñó (Dios la guarde), y puede testificarlo.

Acuérdome que en estos tiempos, siendo mi golosina la que es ordinaria en aquella edad, me abstenía de comer queso, porque oí decir que hacía rudos , y podía conmigo más el deseo de saber que el de comer, siendo éste tan poderoso en los niños. Teniendo yo después como seis o siete años, y sabiendo ya leer y escribir, con todas las otras habilidades de labores y costuras que deprenden las mujeres, oí decir que había Universidad y Escuelas en que se estudiaban las ciencias, en Méjico; y apenas lo oí cuando empecé a matar a mi madre con instantes e importunos ruegos sobre que, mudándome el traje, me enviase a Méjico, a casa de unos deudos que tenía, para estudiar y

live with relatives, to study and be tutored at the University. She would not permit it, and she was wise, but I assuaged my disappointment by reading the many and varied books belonging to my grandfather, and there were not enough punishments, nor reprimands, to prevent me from reading: so that when I came to the city many marveled, not so much at my natural wit, as at my memory, and at the amount of learning I had mastered at an age when many have scarcely learned to speak well.

I began to study Latin grammar — in all, I believe, I had no more than twenty lessons — and so intense was my concern that though among women (especially a woman in the flower of her youth) the natural adornment of one's hair is held in such high esteem, I cut off mine to the breadth of some four to six fingers, measuring the place it had reached, and imposing upon myself the condition that if by the time it had again grown to that length I had not learned such and such a thing I had set for myself to learn while my hair was growing, I would again cut it off as punishment for being so slow-witted. And it did happen that my hair grew out and still I had not learned what I had set for myself — because my hair grew quickly and I learned slowly — and in fact I did cut it in punishment for such stupidity: for there seemed to me no cause for a head to be adorned with hair and naked of learning — which was the more desired embellishment. And so I entered the religious order, knowing that life there entailed certain conditions (I refer to superficial, and not fundamental, regards) most repugnant to my nature; but given the total antipathy I felt for marriage, I deemed convent life the least unsuitable and the most honorable I could elect if I were to insure my salvation. Working against that end, first (as, finally, the most important) was the matter of all the trivial aspects of my nature which nourished my pride, such as wishing to live alone, and wishing to have no obligatory occupation that would inhibit the freedom of my studies, nor the sounds of

cursar la Universidad; ella no lo quiso hacer, e hizo muy bien; pero yo despiqué el deseo en leer muchos libros varios que tenía mi abuelo , sin que bastasen castigos ni reprensiones a estorbarlo; de manera que cuando vine a Méjico, se admiraban, no tanto del ingenio, cuanto de la memoria y noticias que tenía en edad que parecía que apenas había tenido tiempo para aprender a hablar.

Empecé a deprender gramática , en que creo no llegaron a veinte las lecciones que tomé; y era tan intenso mi cuidado, que siendo así que en las mujeres—y más en tan florida juventud—es tan apreciable el adorno natural del cabello, yo me cortaba de él cuatro o seis dedos, midiendo hasta dónde llegaba antes e imponiéndome ley de que si cuando volviese a crecer hasta allí no sabía tal o tal cosa que me había propuesto deprender en tanto que crecía, me lo había de volver a cortar en pena de la rudeza. Sucedía así que él crecía y yo no sabía lo propuesto, porque el pelo crecía aprisa y yo aprendía despacio, y con efecto le cortaba en pena de la rudeza, que no me parecía razón que estuviese vestida de cabellos cabeza que estaba tan desnuda de noticias, que era más apetecible adorno. Entréme religiosa, porque aunque conocía que tenía el estado cosas (de las accesorias hablo, no de las formales) muchas repugnantes a mi genio, con todo, para la total negación que tenía al matrimonio, era lo menos desproporcionado y lo más decente que podía elegir en materia de la seguridad que deseaba de mi salvación; a cuyo primer respeto (como al fin más importante) cedieron y sujetaron la cerviz todas las impertinencillas de mi genio, que eran de querer vivir sola; de no querer tener ocupación obligatoria que embarazase la libertad de mi estudio, ni

a community that would intrude upon the peaceful silence of my books. These desires caused me to falter some while in my decision, until certain learned persons enlightened me, explaining that they were temptation, and, with divine favor, I overcame them, and took upon myself the state which now so unworthily I hold. I believed that I was fleeing from myself, but — wretch that I am! — I brought with me my worst enemy, my inclination, which I do not know whether to consider a gift or a punishment from Heaven, for once dimmed and encumbered by the many activities common to Religion, that inclination exploded in me like gunpowder, proving how *privation is the source of appetite.*[13]

I turned again (which is badly put, for I never ceased), I continued, then, in my studious endeavour (which for me was respite during those moments not occupied by my duties) of reading and more reading, of study and more study, with no teachers but my books. Thus I learned how difficult it is to study those soulless letters, lacking a human voice or the explication of a teacher. But I suffered this labor happily for my love of learning. Oh, had it only been for love of God, which were proper, how worthwhile it would have been! I strove mightily to elevate these studies, to dedicate them to His service, as the goal to which I aspired was to study Theology — it seeming to me debilitating for a Catholic not to know everything in this life of the Divine Mysteries that can be learned through natural means — and, being a nun and not a layperson, it was seemly that I profess my vows to learning through ecclesiastical channels; and especially, being a daughter of a Saint Jerome and a Saint Paula, it was essential that such erudite parents not be shamed by a witless daughter. This is the argument I proposed to myself, and it seemed to me well-reasoned. It was, however (and this cannot be denied) merely glorification and approbation of my inclination, and enjoyment of it offered as justification. And so I continued, as I have said, directing the course of my studies toward the peak of Sa-

rumor de comunidad que impidiese el sosegado silencio de mis libros. Esto me hizo vacilar algo en la determinación, hasta que alumbrándome personas doctas de que era tentación, la vencí con el favor divino y tomé el estado que tan indignamente tengo. Pensé yo que huía de mí misma, pero, ¡miserable de mí!, trájeme a mí conmigo y traje mi mayor enemigo en esta inclinación, que no sé determinar si por prenda o castigo me dio el Cielo, pues de apagarse o embarazarse con tanto ejercicio que la religión tiene, reventaba como pólvora, y se verificaba en mí el *privatio est causa appetitus* .

Volví (mal dije, pues nunca cesé); proseguí, digo, a la estudiosa tarea (que para mí era descanso en todos los ratos que sobraban a mi obligación) de leer y más leer, de estudiar y más estudiar, sin más maestro que los mismos libros. Ya se ve cuán duro es estudiar en aquellos caracteres sin alma, careciendo de la voz viva y explicación del maestro; pues todo este trabajo sufría yo muy gustosa por amor de las letras. ¡Oh, si hubiese sido por amor de Dios, que era lo acertado, cuánto hubiera merecido! Bien que yo procuraba elevarlo cuanto podía y dirigirlo a su servicio, porque el fin a que aspiraba era a estudiar Teología, pareciéndome menguada inhabilidad, siendo católica, no saber todo lo que en esta vida se puede alcanzar, por medios naturales, de los divinos misterios; y que siendo monja y no seglar debía, por el estado eclesiástico, profesar letras; y más siendo hija de un San Jerónimo y de una Santa Paula , que era degenerar de tan doctos padres ser idiota la hija. Esto me proponía yo de mí misma y me parecía razón; si no es que era (y eso es lo más cierto) lisonjear y aplaudir a mi propia inclinación, proponiéndola como obligatorio su propio gusto.

Con esto proseguí, dirigiendo siempre, como he dicho, los pasos de mi estudio a la cumbre de la Sagrada

cred Theology, it seeming necessary to me, in order to scale those heights, to climb the steps of the human sciences and arts; for how could one undertake the study of the Queen of Sciences if first one had not come to know her servants?

How, without Logic, could I be apprised of the general and specific way in which the Holy Scripture is written? How, without Rhetoric, could I understand its figures, its tropes, its locutions? How, without Physics, so many innate questions concerning the nature of animals, their sacrifices, wherein exist so many symbols, many already declared, many still to be discovered? How should I know whether Saul's being refreshed by the sound of David's harp was due to the virtue and natural power of Music, or to a transcendent power God wished to place in David? How, without Arithmetic, could one understand the computations of the years, days, months, hours, those mysterious weeks communicated by Gabriel to Daniel, and others for whose understanding one must know the nature, concordance, and properties of numbers? How, without Geometry, could one measure the Holy Arc of the Covenant and the Holy City of Jerusalem, whose mysterious measures are foursquare in their dimensions, as well as the miraculous proportions of all their parts? How, without Architecture, could one know the great Temple of Solomon, of which God Himself was the Author who conceived the disposition and the design, and the Wise King but the overseer who executed it, of which temple there was no foundation without mystery, no column without symbolism, no cornice without allusion, no architrave without significance; and similarly others of its parts, of which the least fillet was never intended solely for the service and complement of Art, but as symbol of greater things? How, without great knowledge of the laws and parts of which History is comprised, could one understand historical Books? Or those recapitulations in which many times what happened first is seen in the narrated account to have happened later?

Teología; pareciéndome preciso, para llegar a ella, subir por los escalones de las ciencias y artes humanas; porque ¿cómo entenderá el estilo de la Reina de las Ciencias quien aún no sabe el de las ancilas? ¿Cómo sin Lógica sabría yo los métodos generales y particulares con que está escrita la Sagrada Escritura? ¿Cómo sin Retórica entendería sus figuras, tropos y locuciones? ¿Cómo sin Física, tantas cuestiones naturales de las naturalezas de los animales de los sacrificios, donde se simbolizan tantas cosas ya declaradas y otras muchas que hay? ¿Cómo si el sanar Saúl al sonido del arpa de David fue virtud y fuerza natural de la música, o sobrenatural que Dios quiso poner en David? ¿Cómo sin Aritmética se podrán entender tantos cómputos de años, de días, de meses, de horas, de hebdómadas tan misteriosas como las de Daniel, y otras para cuya inteligencia es necesario saber las naturalezas, concordancias y propiedades de los números? ¿Cómo sin Geometría se podrán medir el Arca Santa del Testamento y la Ciudad Santa de Jerusalén, cuyas misteriosas mensuras hacen un cubo con todas sus dimensiones, y aquel repartimiento proporcional de todas sus partes tan maravilloso? ¿Cómo sin Arquitectura, el gran Templo de Salomón, donde fue el mismo Dios el artífice que dio la disposición y la traza, y el Sabio Rey sólo fue sobrestante que la ejecutó; donde no había basa sin misterio, columna sin símbolo, cornisa sin alusión, arquitrabe sin significado; y así de otras sus partes, sin que el más mínimo filete estuviese sólo por el servicio y complemento del Arte, sino simbolizando cosas mayores? ¿Cómo sin grande conocimiento de reglas y partes de que consta la Historia se entenderán los libros historiales? Aquellas recapitulaciones en que muchas veces se pospone en la narración lo que en el hecho sucedió

How, without great learning in Canon and Civil Law, could one understand Legal Books? How, without great erudition, could one apprehend the secular histories of which the Holy Scripture makes mention, such as the many customs of the Gentiles, their many rites, their many ways of speaking? How without the abundant laws and lessons of the Holy Fathers could one understand the obscure lesson of the Prophets? And without being expert in Music, how could one understand the exquisite precision of the musical proportions that grace so many Scriptures, particularly those in which Abraham beseeches God in defense of the Cities, asking whether He would spare the place were there but fifty just men therein; and then Abraham reduced that number to five less than fifty, forty-five, which is a ninth, and is as Mi to Re; then to forty, which is a tone, and is as Re to Mi; from forty to thirty, which is a diastesseron, the interval of the perfect fourth; from thirty to twenty, which is the perfect fifth; and from twenty to ten, which is the octave, the diapason; and as there are no further harmonic proportions, made no further reductions. How might one understand this without Music? And there in the Book of Job, God says to Job: *Shalt thou be able to join together the shining stars the Pleiades, or canst thou stop the turning about of Arcturus? Canst thou bring forth the day star in its time, and make the evening star to rise upon the children of the earth?*[14] Which message, without knowledge of Astrology, would be impossible to apprehend. And not only these noble sciences; there is no applied art that is not mentioned. And, finally, in consideration of the Book that comprises all books, and the Science in which all sciences are embraced, and for whose comprehension all sciences serve, and even after knowing them all (which we now see is not easy, nor even possible), there is one condition that takes precedence over all the rest, which is uninterrupted prayer and purity of life, that one may entreat of God that purgation of spirit and illumination of mind necessary for the understanding

primero. ¿Cómo sin grande noticia de ambos Derechos podrán entenderse los libros legales? ¿Cómo sin grande erudición tantas cosas de historias profanas, de que hace mención la Sagrada Escritura; tantas costumbres de gentiles, tantos ritos, tantas maneras de hablar? ¿Cómo sin muchas reglas y lección de Santos Padres se podrá entender la oscura locución de los Profetas? Pues sin ser muy perito en la Música, ¿cómo se entenderán aquellas proporciones musicales y sus primores que hay en tantos lugares, especialmente en aquellas peticiones que hizo a Dios Abraham , por las Ciudades, de que si perdonaría habiendo cincuenta justos, y de este número bajó a cuarenta y cinco, que es sesquinona y es como de mi a re; de aquí a cuarenta, que es sesquioctava y es como de re a mi; de aquí a treinta, que es sesquitercia, que es la del diatesarón; de aquí a veinte, que es la proporción sesquiáltera, que es la del diapente; de aquí a diez, que es la dupla, que es el diapasón; y como no hay más proporciones armónicas no pasó de ahí? Pues ¿cómo se podrá entender esto sin Música? Allá en el Libro de Job le dice Dios: *Numquid coniungere valebis micantes stellas Pleiadas, aut gyrum Arcturi poteris dissipare? Numquid producis Luciferum in tempore suo, et Vesperum super filios terrae consurgere facis?* , cuyos términos, sin noticia de Astrología, será imposible entender. Y no sólo estas nobles ciencias; pero no hay arte mecánica que no mencione. Y en fin, ¿cómo el Libro que comprende todos los libros, y la Ciencia en que se incluyen todas las ciencias, para cuya inteligencia todas sirven? Y después de saberlas todas (que ya se ve que no es fácil, ni aun posible), pide otra circunstancia más que todo lo dicho, que es una continua oración y pureza de vida, para impetrar de Dios aquella purgación de ánimo e iluminación de

of such elevated matters: and if that be lacking, none of the aforesaid will have been of any purpose.

Of the Angelic Doctor Saint Thomas the Church affirms: *When reading the most difficult passages of the Holy Scripture, he joined fast with prayer. And he was wont to say to his companion Brother Reginald that all he knew derived not so much from study or his own labor as from the grace of God.*[15] How then should I — so lacking in virtue and so poorly read — find courage to write? But as I had acquired the rudiments of learning, I continued to study ceaselessly divers subjects, having for none any particular inclination, but for all in general; and having studied some more than others was not owing to preference, but to the chance that more books on certain subjects had fallen into my hands, causing the election of them through no discretion of my own. And as I was not directed by preference, nor, forced by the need to fulfill certain scholarly requirements, constrained by time in the pursuit of any subject, I found myself free to study numerous topics at the same time, or to leave some for others; although in this scheme some order was observed, for some I deigned study and others diversion, and in the latter I found respite from the former. From which it follows that though I have studied many things I know nothing, as some have inhibited the learning of others. I speak specifically of the practical aspect of those arts that allow practice, because it is clear that when the pen moves the compass must lie idle, and while the harp is played the organ is stilled, *et sic de caeteris.* And because much practice is required of one who would acquire facility, none who divides his interest among various exercises may reach perfection. Whereas in the formal and theoretical arts the contrary is true, and I would hope to persuade all with my experience, which is that one need not inhibit the other, but, in fact, each may illuminate and open the way to others, by nature of their variations and their hidden links, which were placed in this universal chain by the wisdom of their Au-